MAMBOS! SAMBAS! RHUMBAS!

Esta libro contiene:

Y0-DBV-568

BRAZIL

Words and Music by S.K. RUSSELL
and ARY BARROSO

MAMBOS! SAMBAS! RHUMBAS!

Piano • Canto • Guitarra
Piano • Vocal • Guitar

ISBN 0-634-01347-5

HAL•LEONARD®
CORPORATION
7777 W. BLUEMOUND RD. P.O. BOX 13819 MILWAUKEE, WI 53213

Visit Hal Leonard Online at
www.halleonard.com

THE BREEZE AND I

Words by AL STILLMAN
Music by ERNESTO LECUONA

THE CONSTANT RAIN
(Chove Chuva)

Original Words and Music by JORGE BEN
English Words by NORMAN GIMBEL

14

CUANTO LE GUSTA

Original Words and Music by
GABRIEL RUIZ
English Words by
RAY GILBERT

some - one said they just came back from some - where, _____ a

friend of mine that I don't e - ven know. _____ He

said there's lots of fun if we can get there. _____ If

that's the case, that's the place, the

A DEEPER SHADE OF SOUL

Words and Music by
RAY BARRETTO

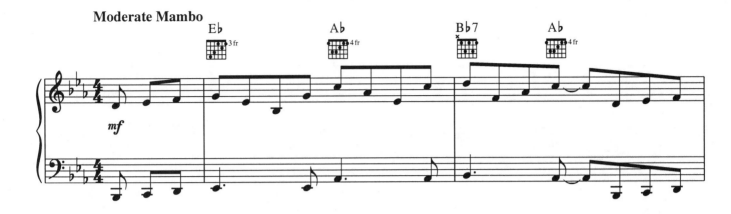

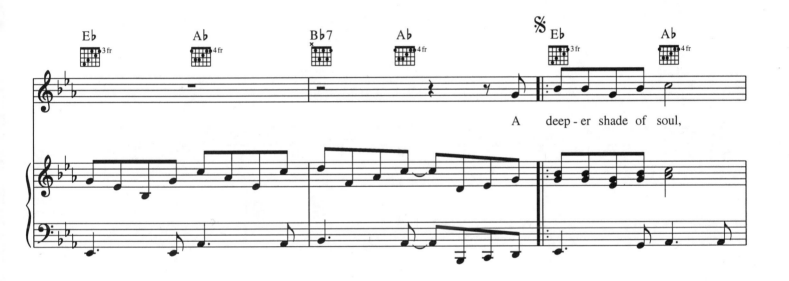

A deep-er shade of soul,

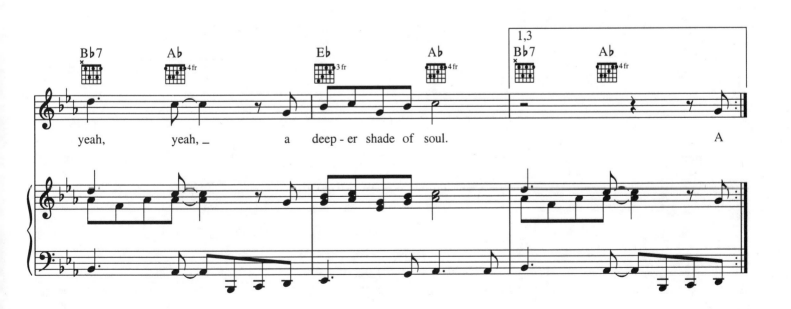

yeah, yeah, _ a deep-er shade of soul.
A

23

CUMANÁ

Words by HAROLD SPINA and ROC HILLMAN
Music by BARCLAY ALLEN

EL CUMBANCHERO

Words and Music by
RAFAEL HERNANDEZ

MAMBO #8

Words and Music by
DÁMASO PÉREZ PRADO

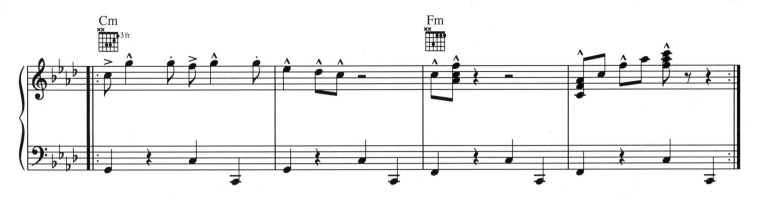

(Spoken:)
Uno,   *dos,*   *tres,*   *cuatro,*   *cinco,*

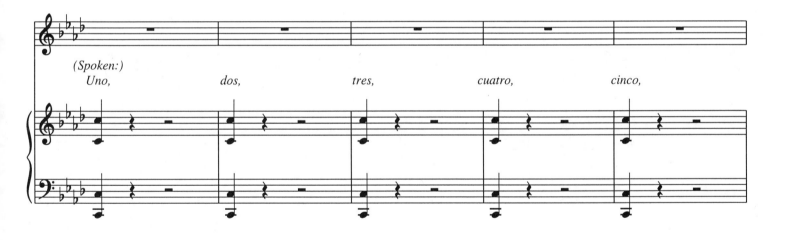

seis,   *siete,*   *ocho,*   *mam - bo!*

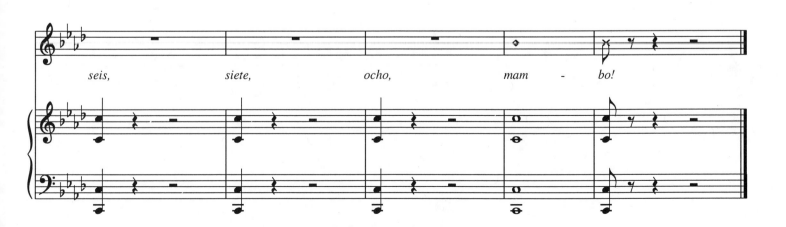

HARD HANDS

Words and Music by
RAY BARRETTO

G7

N.C.

D.S. al Coda
(with repeats)

I don't know what to do now.
Watch out, his soul

has caught on fire.

CODA

(Spoken:) Hard hands,

MAMBO JAMBO
(Que Rico El Mambo)

English Words by RAYMOND KARL and CHARLIE TOWNE
Original Words and Music by DAMASO PEREZ PRADO

42

MAMBO #5

Words and Music by
DÁMASO PÉREZ PRADO

Moderately

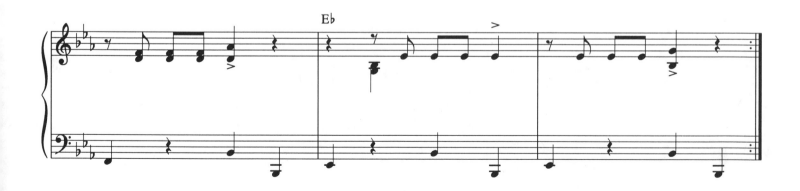

Si   Si   Si   yo qui - ero   Mam - bo!

MAMBO SWING

Words and Music by
SCOTTY MORRIS

Moderate Latin beat

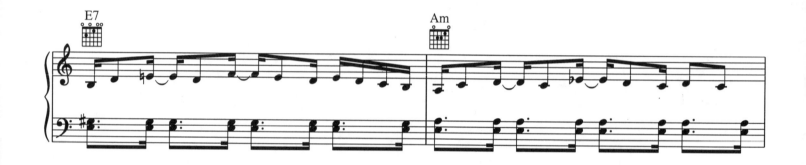

49

Swing-in' through the jun — gle,   I have sailed the Sev -en Seas. ___
Fires ___ in the cit - y.   There was danc -ing in the streets. ___

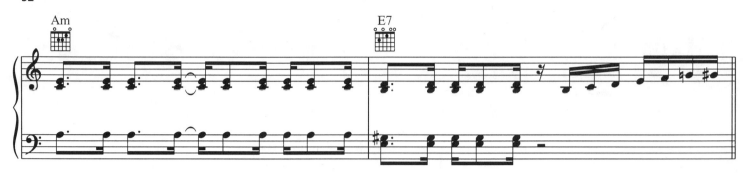

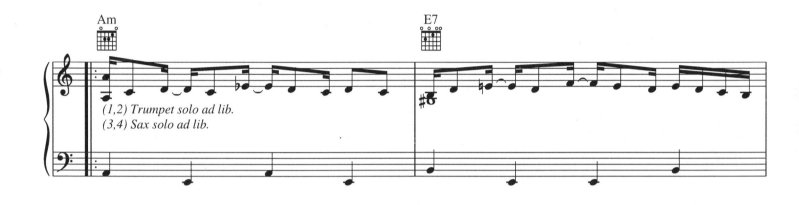

(1,2) Trumpet solo ad lib.
(3,4) Sax solo ad lib.

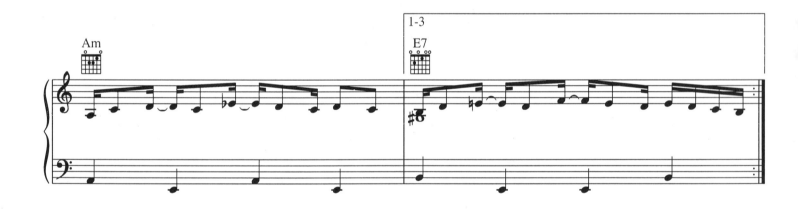

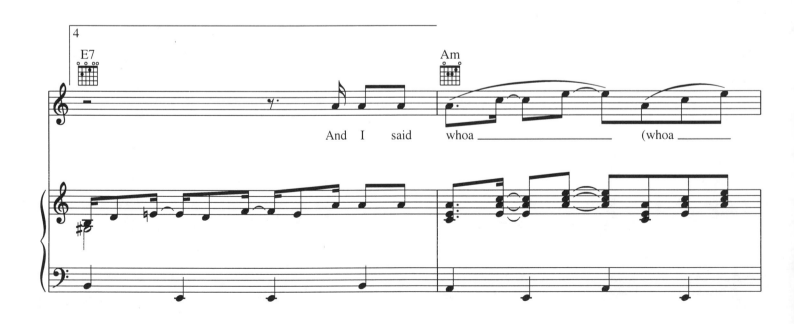

And I said whoa _____ (whoa _____

MAÑANA

Words and Music by PEGGY LEE
and DAVE BARBOUR

Additional Lyrics

3. Oh, once I had some money but I gave it to my friend.
   He said he'd pay me double, it was only for a lend.
   But he said a little later that the horse she was so slow.
   Why he gave the horse my money is something I don't know.

4. My brother took his suitcase and he went away to school.
   My father said he only learn'd to be a silly fool.
   My father said that I should learn to make a chili pot.
   But then I burn'd the house down the chili was too hot.

5. The window she is broken and the rain is coming in.
   If someone doesn't fix it I'll be soaking to my skin.
   But if we wait a day or two the rain may go away.
   And we don't need a window on such a sunny day.

MIAMI BEACH RUMBA

Words by ALBERT GAMSE
Music by IRVING FIELDS

Rhumba

I start-ed out to go to Hai - ti,
That's where the or-ang-es are round-er,
Soon I was at Mi - am - i
That's where the win-ter days are

Beach.
warm.

There, not so ver - y far from Hai - ti,
That's where I caught a hun-dred pound-er,

60

MIS AMORES

By BEBU SILVETTI
and ROBERTO LIVI

64

MY SHAWL

English Lyric by STANLEY ADAMS
Spanish Lyric by PEDRO BERRIOS
Music by XAVIER CUGAT

68

O PATO
(The Duck)

Words and Music by
JAYME SILVA and NEUZA TEIXIERA

Moderate Samba

O pa-
-to __ vi- nha can-ta-do a-le-gra-men-te, quen, quen,_
__ qua-do o mar-re-co sor-ri-den-te pe-diu

PAPA LOVES MAMBO

Words and Music by AL HOFFMAN,
DICK MANNING and BIX REICHNER

Pa - pa loves mam - bo.

Ma - ma loves mam - bo.

Look at 'em sway _ with it,

get - tin' so gay _ with it, shout - in' "O - lay!" _ with it wow!

THE PEANUT VENDOR
(El Manisero)

English Words by MARION SUNSHINE and L. WOLFE GILBERT
Music and Spanish Words by MOISES SIMONS

PORQUE TÚ LO QUIERES

Words and Music by
MARIO CLAVELL

Rumba - Guaracha

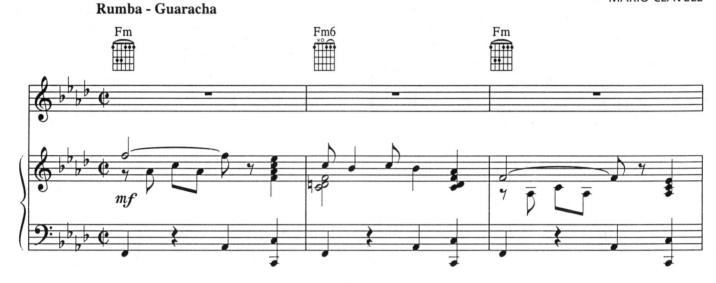

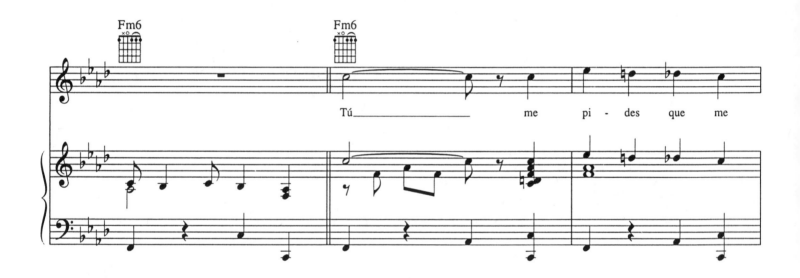

Tú_____ me pi - des que me

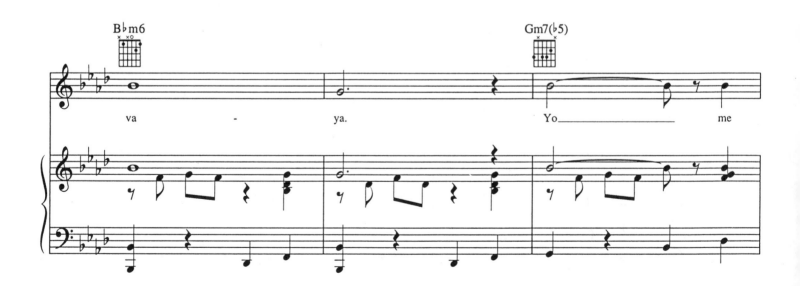

va - ya. Yo_____ me

SAMBA DE ORFEU

Words by ANTONIO MARIA
Music by LUIZ BONFA

SAMBA PA TI

Words and Music by
CARLOS SANTANA

SÓ DANÇO SAMBA

(Jazz 'n' Samba)
from the film COPACABANA PALACE

English Lyric by NORMAN GIMBEL
Original Text by VINICIUS DE MORAES
Music by ANTONIO CARLOS JOBIM

SOMEONE TO LIGHT UP MY LIFE
(Se Todos Fossem Iguais A Voce)

English Lyric by GENE LEES
Original Text by VINICIUS DE MORAES
Music by ANTONIO CARLOS JOBIM

98

TICO TICO
(Tico No Fuba)

Words and Music by ZEQUINHA ABREU,
ALOYSIO OLIVEIRA and ERVIN DRAKE

Bright Samba

Oh ti-co-ti-co tick! __ Oh ti-co-ti-co tock! __ This ti-co
O ti-co-ti-co tá, __ tá ou-tra vez a - qui, __ o ti-co-

ti-co he's the cuck-oo in my clock. And when he says: "Cuck - oo!" __ he means it's
ti-co-tá co-men-do o meu fu - bá. Si o ti-co-ti-co tem, __ tem que se a-

time to woo; __ It's "Ti-co time" for all the lov-ers in the
li - men - tar, __ Que vá co - mer u - mas mi - nho-cas no po-

VEN Y DAME UN POCO MÁS

By BEBU SILVETTI
and SYLVIA IBANEZ

Bus-

can-do un a - mor sin - ce - ro tu ve a ven-tu - ras que no re-cuer-
ve - ces yo me cre-í - a que e - ra to - das a-quel que-rí-

107

SPEAK LOW

from the Musical Production ONE TOUCH OF VENUS

Words by OGDEN NASH
Music by KURT WEILL

111